21st
Century
Skills Library

REAL WORLD MATH: NATURAL DISASTERS
TORNADOES

BY TAMRA B. ORR

Published in the United States of America by
Cherry Lake Publishing, Ann Arbor, Michigan
www.cherrylakepublishing.com

Content Adviser
Jack Williams
Founding editor of the *USA Today* weather page and author of *The AMS Weather Book: The Ultimate Guide to America's Weather*

Math Adviser
Katherine M. Gregory, M.Ed

Photo Credits
Cover and page 1, ©lafoto/Shutterstock, Inc.; page 4, ©deepspacedave/Shutterstock, Inc.; page 6, ©AP Photo/The News Leader, Valerie Mosley; page 8, ©Steshkin Yevgeniy/Shutterstock, Inc.; page 11, ©AP Photo/Daily Oklahoman, Steve Sisney; page 14, ©Reven T.C. Wurman/Alamy; page 20, ©AP Photo/Sue Ogrocki; page 22, ©Jim West/Alamy; page 24, ©shaecardenas/Shutterstock, Inc.; page 27, ©1125089601/Shutterstock, Inc.

Copyright ©2012 by Cherry Lake Publishing
All rights reserved. No part of this book may be reproduced or utilized in any form or by any means without written permission from the publisher.

Library of Congress Cataloging-in-Publication Data
Orr, Tamra.
  Tornadoes/by Tamra B. Orr.
    p. cm.—(Real world math)
  Includes bibliographical references and index.
  ISBN 978-1-61080-326-7 (lib. bdg.)—ISBN 978-1-61080-335-9 (e-book)—
ISBN 978-1-61080-413-4 (pbk.)
  1. Tornadoes—Juvenile literature. 2. Mathematics—Problems, exercises, etc.—
Juvenile literature. I. Title. II. Series.
  QC955.2.077 2012
  551.55'3—dc23   2011034822

Cherry Lake Publishing would like to acknowledge
the work of The Partnership for 21st Century Skills.
Please visit *www.21stcenturyskills.org* for more information.

Printed in the United States of America
Corporate Graphics Inc.
January 2012
CLSP10

TABLE OF CONTENTS

CHAPTER ONE
PANIC IN MISSOURI

May 22, 2011, seemed to be just another normal Sunday in Joplin, Missouri. In the early evening hours, many of the city's 50,000 residents were casually thinking about what to eat for dinner. Some of them might have grown worried about the **ominous**-looking gray sky. After all,

It is never good to see a tornado on the horizon.

Missouri was one of the most frequently hit states during tornado season. And by May, 2011 was already one of the nation's worst tornado years in history.

When the tornado alarms went off throughout the city, families headed to their basements and shelters. They knew what to do because many of them had experienced tornadoes before. The U.S. National Weather Service issued warnings to the people of Joplin. They were told that they had only minutes before the tornado would drop down onto the city.

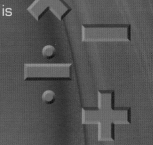

REAL WORLD MATH CHALLENGE

Tornado A is traveling at 30 miles per hour. Tornado B is traveling at 55 mph. Tornado C is traveling at 10 mph. If they maintain the same speeds, how far will each tornado travel in 90 minutes?

(Turn to page 29 for the answer)

The tornado slammed into town at 5:41 p.m. It carved a path 6 miles (9.7 kilometers) long and more than 0.5 miles (0.8 km) wide. More than one-quarter of the city was destroyed, and at least 2,000 buildings were leveled. The **twister** blew out every window in the city hospital. Flying glass cut many patients. Some people sitting in the waiting room were sucked out of the windows and hurled outside onto the parking lot. At the fire station, a brick wall toppled over a truck.

The tornado, which exceeded speeds of 200 miles (322 km) per hour, killed 150 people. More than 1,000 people were injured, and hundreds more were missing. By the time it passed, the tornado had become the deadliest single twister in more than half a century. It was the eighth deadliest in U.S. history.

The people of Joplin combed through the wreckage of their homes and businesses. They tried to pick up the pieces

Many Joplin residents lost their homes to the tornado.

LEARNING & INNOVATION SKILLS

Tornado warnings save a lot of lives, but they could save more. Current warning systems are better than they once were. Still, they provide an average of only 13 minutes' warning, and they turn out to be false alarms roughly 75 percent of the time. A number of researchers, scientists, and inventors are searching for ways to make the warning systems more effective. A team of researchers from Colorado State University installed a network of eight small radar transmitters in Dallas, Texas. The transmitters are designed to scan the skies for potential tornadoes. From the data collected, weather forecasters can determine if a tornado is forming and how it might behave. This system updates every 30 seconds. That's 5 to 10 times faster than the usual radar systems. This speedy feedback can give warning systems more time to let people know they are in danger.

of their shattered lives. The tornado's brutal force reminded the world of Mother Nature's power. And it was a reminder that when storm clouds gather overhead, it's time to be on guard. A twister might be in the making.

CHAPTER TWO
THE BIRTH OF A TWISTER

L ightning flashes and thunder rumbles overhead. Clouds grow dark with rain, and the breeze picks up. A thunderstorm is rolling into the area. This is a common

Many tornadoes begin with thunderstorms.

event in most parts of the United States during spring and summer. Soon, a cooling rain will fall. A strong wind will blow, and then, eventually, the storm will fade away.

This is the way most thunderstorms behave. Sometimes, however, a thunderstorm brings with it something much scarier—a tornado.

Tornadoes can occur in all parts of the world. India, Argentina, and Bangladesh are countries that have experienced a number of severe tornadoes over the years. But three out of four tornadoes happen in the United States. Every state has had at least one. The most likely area to get a tornado is the section of the country known as Tornado Alley. This includes North and South Dakota, Nebraska, Kansas, Oklahoma, Texas, Louisiana, Arkansas, Missouri, Illinois, Iowa, Minnesota, and part of Colorado.

Tornado Alley experiences the highest number of tornadoes. However, more people are killed by tornadoes in the Southeast region of the country. Between 1950 and 1997, Alabama, Arkansas, Louisiana, Mississippi, Georgia, Florida, Tennessee, North Carolina, and South Carolina experienced 9,178 tornadoes, in which 1,648 people died. During that time, Texas, Oklahoma, Kansas, Nebraska, and Missouri had 13,808 tornadoes. Those storms took the lives of 1,132 people. The reasons for the difference include type of housing, geography, and higher populations in the Southeast. Also, tornadoes in the Southeast tend to hit at night. Nighttime tornadoes are harder to see, and people may sleep through sirens or not be able to react quickly.

LEARNING &
INNOVATION SKILLS

The Verification of the Origins of Rotation in Tornadoes Experiment (VORTEX) is the largest and most ambitious effort ever made to understand tornadoes. More than 100 scientists and 40 science and support vehicles participated in two major studies. VORTEX1 was conducted in 1994 and 1995. Several smaller studies were undertaken from 1996 to 2008. VORTEX1 used about 18 vehicles equipped with high-tech instruments. They measured and analyzed the weather around a tornado. For the first time, the entire life cycle of a tornado was documented.

VORTEX2 was conducted from 2009 to 2010. It studied why some tornadoes are violent and long lasting while others are weak and short-lived. Researchers also wanted to learn more about the structure of tornadoes. They hoped to find out how strong the winds near the ground are and exactly how they do damage. An **armada** of vehicles and high-tech instruments roamed more than 10,000 miles (16,000 km) across the central and southern plains of the United States. They followed tornadoes as they traveled. Researchers are analyzing the collected data. They hope to be better able to forecast tornadoes and increase the warning time to residents living in the path of a twister.

The VORTEX2 project used special equipment to measure wind speed, air pressure, and other important weather information.

How is a twister born? It starts with the energy of a thunderstorm. All thunderstorms begin with warm, humid air rising from the ground. As the rising air cools, the humidity **condenses** to form lumpy **cumulus** clouds. Some of these clouds grow into individual thunderstorm **cells** or groups of cells. They hold lightning, thunder, rain, and cooling breezes before dying out. Sometimes, these will produce relatively weak tornadoes. The strongest tornadoes come from a kind of thunderstorm that lives up to its name: **supercell**.

Supercells are much stronger than ordinary thunderstorm cells, and they last much longer. They form when the winds moving from ground level up to the **jet stream**—located more than 25,000 feet (7,620 meters) above—blow in different directions. This gives the rising air a spinning motion. How fast that wind spins determines the intensity, strength, and danger of any tornado that emerges from the supercell. This circle of spinning air can be 10 miles (16 km) across. If it shrinks to less than 1 mile (1.6 km) across, it speeds up.

The fast-spinning air forms a **funnel cloud**. As the funnel cloud grows stronger, it begins to stretch down to the ground. Some never make it all the way down. Those that do officially become tornadoes. Sometimes they touch the earth for a few seconds. Sometimes they remain for hours. They have the power to rip off roofs, toss trucks and cars, and flatten homes and other buildings. They move across the ground, creating a path of destruction.

REAL WORLD MATH CHALLENGE

The chart below lists the 10 deadliest tornadoes in U.S. history. What is the total number of deaths caused by these tornadoes?

Date	Location	Number of Deaths
March 18, 1925	Missouri, Illinois, and Indiana	625
May 7, 1840	Mississippi	317
May 27, 1896	Missouri and Illinois	255
April 5, 1936	Mississippi	233
April 6, 1936	Georgia	203
April 9, 1947	Texas, Oklahoma, and Kansas	181
April 24, 1908	Mississippi	143
May 23, 2011	Missouri	117
June 12, 1899	Wisconsin	117
June 8, 1953	Michigan	115

(Turn to page 29 for the answer)

CHAPTER THREE

DO THE MATH: TORNADO FACTS AND FICTION

I n the movie *The Wizard of Oz*, Dorothy's house rides on a tornado from Kansas to the Land of Oz. There have long been stories and legends told about twisters. But you need to

Storm chasers load up their trucks with equipment for measuring and recording tornadoes.

know the difference between tornado fact and fiction. It's the only way to stay safe in dangerous weather. Read the following statements and decide if they are true or not. Then read on to see if you were right!

1. Tornadoes are so big and loud that it's impossible to not know one is coming.
2. The safest place to be in a tornado is the southwest corner of a basement.
3. Thunderstorms with the potential to cause tornadoes are usually accompanied by large amounts of hail and lightning.
4. Tornadoes are not able to cross over water.
5. Most tornado deaths occur when people are buried in collapsed buildings or hit by flying **debris**.
6. People and fragile items have been lifted up by a tornado and set down without injury or damage.
7. The larger the tornado, the more dangerous it is.
8. Tornadoes can come in different colors.
9. Driving away from a twister is wiser than taking shelter from one.
10. Tornadoes can occur at any time of night or day, and during the fall and winter seasons.

Now, let's find out how much you know about tornadoes!

1. Tornadoes are so big and loud that it's impossible to not know one is coming.
FICTION. You often cannot hear a tornado until it is almost upon you, especially if rain, wind, and thunder accompany it. Tornadoes cannot always be seen, either. They can hide in large storm clouds and form a funnel that touches down in mere seconds.

LIFE & CAREER SKILLS

If you heard a tornado warning, would you rush to look out the window instead of heading for the basement? Do you watch movies about twisters and wish you could have been there to experience it firsthand? If so, you might be interested in becoming a **storm chaser**. For more than 50 years, people have chased storms. Some storm chasers are scientists in search of knowledge. Others are thrill seekers wanting to witness nature's power up close. Some storm chasers work for television and radio stations. They report or film the event for their audiences. Mike Hollingshead and Eric Nguyen are storm chasers and authors. In their book, *The Storm Chasers: Adventures in Tornado Alley*, they write, "In storm chasing, you have the chance to see a pageant of power and elegant form unfold before your eyes, even in the absence of the ultimate: a tornado."

2. The safest place to be in a tornado is the southwest corner of a basement. FICTION. People once believed this was good advice, but it has since been shown to be false. Instead, the best place to be is in a protected inner room in a basement or on the lowest floor possible. Stay away from exterior walls and windows.

3. Thunderstorms with the potential to cause tornadoes are usually accompanied by large amounts of hail and lightning. FACT. The most powerful thunderstorms are the ones that tend to produce tornadoes. Typically, these storms also have more than the average amount of lightning plus large hailstones.

4. Tornadoes are not able to cross over water. FICTION. Tornadoes can easily cross water. A **waterspout** is a funnel cloud that swirls above a body of water. The water seen in the funnel is water droplets formed by condensation.

5. Most tornado deaths occur when people are buried in collapsed buildings or hit by flying debris. FACT. Injuries or deaths from a tornado are rarely because of the storm itself. People are most often injured or killed by falling buildings and debris. Often, people are harmed by being inside a vehicle or mobile home that has been flipped over.

6. People and fragile items have been lifted up by a tornado and set down without injury or damage. FACT. Funnel clouds have picked up everything from people to china dishware and then set them down somewhere else, without more than a scratch. Sometimes they are set down miles away.

7. The larger the tornado, the more dangerous it is. FICTION. Although wider tornadoes certainly look more threatening, they are not always the most dangerous. Long, thin, ropey funnel clouds can be very powerful. A tornado's strength comes not from its size but from the speed of its winds.

8. Tornadoes can come in different colors. FACT. The color of a tornado comes mainly from whatever it is sucking up from the ground. It can be gray or black or red. It depends on the color of the soil and what debris is flying around inside the cloud. Some tornadoes are invisible, at least for a while, before they pick up dust and dirt.

9. Driving away from a twister is wiser than taking shelter from one. FICTION. If you were driving at the exact correct angle, it's possible that you could outrun a tornado in a car. But tornadoes often change direction. In addition, you are likely to encounter pouring rain that limits your visibility. There might be downed power lines and telephone poles. These dangerous obstacles create traffic jams that would slow you down and increase your risk of an accident.

10. Tornadoes can occur at any time of night or day, and during the fall and winter seasons. FACT. Although tornadoes usually strike between 3:00 and 9:00 p.m., they can hit at any hour of the day or night. Also, while most twisters strike in spring and summer, they can occur in autumn and winter.

REAL WORLD MATH CHALLENGE

The Enhanced Fujita Scale, also known as the EF-scale, measures the intensity of a tornado. The chart below shows each type of tornado in the scale. Fill in the chart's missing wind speeds by converting between miles per hour and kilometers per hour.

(Hint: 1 mile = 1.6 kilometers)

Scale	Description	Wind Speed (miles per hour/mph)	Wind speed (kilometers per hour/kph)
EF0	Light damage to trees, chimneys, and billboards	65–85	??
EF1	Moderate damage: autos pushed off the road and mobile homes moved	86–110	138–176
EF2	Considerable damage: roofs torn off houses, mobile homes ruined, and large trees uprooted	??	178–216
EF3	Severe damage: houses torn apart, trees uprooted, cars lifted off the ground	136–165	218–264
EF4	Devastating damage: objects and debris are deadly	??	266–320
EF5	Incredible damage: structures lifted and carried away, cars hurled wildly. Roughly 2 percent of tornadoes reach this level.	More than 200	??

(Turn to page 29 for the answers)

CHAPTER FOUR

DO THE MATH: HELP FROM THE EXPERTS

W hen people need to know if a tornado will be forming, they turn to the experts. The Storm Prediction Center (SPC) in Norman, Oklahoma, is one place where

Experts at the Storm Prediction Center try to predict where and when tornadoes will appear.

experts are found. The organization works to provide accurate forecasts and watches for severe thunderstorms and tornadoes in the United States. The SPC also keeps track of heavy rain and snowfall, as well as fire events throughout the country. You can visit the SPC's Web site at *www.spc.noaa.gov*.

REAL WORLD MATH CHALLENGE

The following chart provides data about 148 tornadoes that occurred over a 16-hour time period. Using the data in the chart, answer the questions below.

Number of Tornadoes	Number of States Affected	Deaths
148	13	315

a. On average, how many people were killed per tornado?

b. On average, how many tornadoes hit each state?

(Turn to page 29 for the answers)

The SPC issues about 1,000 tornado watches per year. But tornado warnings are issued by the local National Weather Service offices. A "watch" indicates that the weather is favorable for the formation of a twister. A "warning" means that conditions have worsened or a funnel cloud has been sighted in the area by either radar or a person.

Typically, a warning will start with a blaring sound to get people's attention. Then it usually states:

"The National Weather Service in [nearest city] has issued a tornado warning for [counties affected] until [time]. At [time], National Weather Service Doppler radar indicated a tornado located [exact location] and moving [direction and speed]. This dangerous storm will be near [city] around [time]. Locations in the warning include [list counties]. Take cover now. Move to an interior room on the lowest floor of a sturdy building. Avoid windows. If in a mobile home, a vehicle, or outdoors, move to the closest substantial shelter and protect yourself from flying debris. Cover your head with pillows and blankets."

Tornado shelters are often marked by signs so they can be found easily.

When a warning like this is issued, it is time to pay attention and get to safety!

21ST CENTURY CONTENT

Researchers at the Wind Science & Engineering Center at Texas Tech University have had a blast testing in-residence tornado shelters. An in-residence shelter is a windowless room within a house, such as a closet, utility room, or bathroom. Family members can go there to escape a passing tornado. The greatest danger of a tornado is flying debris. So researchers tested the strength of walls, roofs, and doors to see if they could handle being hit by debris. They got a 2 x 4-inch (5 x 10-centimeter) timber plank weighing about 15 pounds (6.8 kilograms). The plank was placed into a compressed air cannon. It was then shot into different types of materials. If the plank was being tested on walls and doors, it was shot from the cannon at 100 miles (161 km) per hour. It was shot at 67 miles (108 km) per hour for roofs and ceilings. The results showed that in-residence shelters constructed with 6- or 8-inch (15.2 or 20.3 cm) concrete masonry held up best. Structures made of plywood and steel also performed well. Special doors made of two sheets of ¾-inch (2 cm) plywood glued together and covered with sheet steel proved to be the most resistant.

CHAPTER FIVE
TAKE COVER!

Weather forecasters are hard at work finding new ways of detecting tornadoes faster. But you still need to be prepared and know exactly what to do if a tornado is coming.

Storm shelters are built underground so they can't be knocked over by strong winds or debris.

People who live in areas where tornadoes occur frequently need to pay close attention to weather reports and changing weather conditions. They should watch the skies. Approaching storms may have green-tinted skies, large hail, thunder and lightning, and dark clouds. Know where the closest shelter, such as a basement or special storm cellar, is and how to get there. Power outages often occur before a warning can be issued, so having a battery-operated radio available is an important safety step. Storing clean water and simple snacks in a family shelter is also a wise idea.

Some people do not have a shelter built inside their home. They might consider building a storm cellar or **underground excavation**. It should be constructed on the property, but away from the house. That way, it won't be blocked by debris if a tornado destroys the house. How large the shelter is depends on how many people will be using it. For example, a shelter that is 8 feet long x 6 feet wide x 7 feet high (2.4 x 1.8 x 2.1 m) can fit eight people. Reinforced concrete is considered one of the most effective building materials for shelters. The shelter should be equipped with a flashlight and tools such as a hammer, pliers, and screwdrivers.

When a tornado warning is announced on television or the radio, it's time to take shelter immediately. For those who are inside buildings, it's best to take shelter on the lowest level. Stay away from any exterior walls and windows. If caught outside, people should go to a nearby ditch. Avoid any bridges or overpasses.

Once the tornado has passed, safety is still an important issue. Downed electric lines, burst gas lines, and broken glass present danger. In addition, people are often unable to return to their homes. Many people have to stay in shelters or other locations for weeks or even months. Utilities such as electricity and telephones may not work for a while. Clean water and food may be unavailable until help arrives.

Unlike some natural disasters, tornadoes usually come with a warning, even if it is a brief one. Learn to watch for possible signs of a twister. Listen to weather reports. Preparing for the worst will help keep people safe.

21ST CENTURY CONTENT

Is it possible to build a tornado-proof home or tornado-proof products? Possibly. Although wood, steel, and concrete are no match for a powerful tornado, other products might be. A fabric called Concrete Cloth makes strong shelters because it becomes rigid when water is added to it. Kevlar is typically used to make bulletproof vests. It could also be used to make protective clothing. Carbon fiber has been used to manufacture products such as bicycles, eyeglasses, and airplanes. Bradley Quinn, author of *Design Futures*, explains, "The thinking behind carbon fiber architecture is that it can withstand earthquakes. It would be more flexible in the wind than regular structures."

Weather sirens make loud noises to let people know that a tornado has been sighted in the area.

REAL WORLD MATH CHALLENGE

The following chart shows the average number of tornadoes in 10 U.S. states from 1961 to 1990. Using the information in the table, answer the questions below.

State	Average Number of Tornadoes Per Year
Texas	137
Florida	52
Oklahoma	47
Kansas	36
Nebraska	36
Iowa	35
South Dakota	28
Missouri	27
Louisiana	27
Illinois	27

a. If $\frac{2}{3}$ of these twisters are considered weak, how many is that?

b. If $\frac{3}{10}$ of these twisters are considered strong, how many is that?

c. If $\frac{1}{5}$ of these twisters are considered violent, how many is that?

(Turn to page 29 for the answers)

REAL WORLD MATH CHALLENGE ANSWERS

Chapter One

Page 5

Tornado A will travel 45 miles.

90 minutes ÷ 60 minutes per hour = 1.5 hours

30 mph × 1.5 hours = 45 miles

Tornado B will travel 82.5 miles.

55 mph × 1.5 hours = 82.5 miles

Tornado C will travel 15 miles.

10 mph × 1.5 hours = 15 miles

Chapter Two

Page 13

The tornadoes caused a total of 2,306 deaths.

625 + 317 + 255 + 233 + 203 + 181 + 143 + 117 + 117 + 115 = 2,306 total deaths

Chapter Three

Page 19

EF0 winds travel 104 to 136 kph.

65 mph × 1.6 = 104 kph

85 mph × 1.6 = 136 kph

EF2 winds travel 111–135 mph.

178 kph ÷ 1.6 = 111.3 mph

216 kph ÷ 1.6 = 135 mph

EF4 winds travel 166–200 mph.

266 kph ÷ 1.6 = 166.3 mph

320 kph ÷ 1.6 = 200 mph

EF5 winds travel more than 320 kph.

200 mph × 1.6 = 320 kph

Chapter Four

Page 21

An average of around 2 people were killed per tornado.

315 deaths ÷ 148 tornadoes = 2.13 deaths per tornado

About 11 tornadoes hit each state.

148 tornadoes ÷ 13 states = 11.38 tornadoes per state

Chapter Five

Page 28

$301\frac{1}{3}$ tornadoes were weak.

452 total tornadoes × $\frac{2}{3}$ = $\frac{904}{3}$ or $301\frac{1}{3}$

$135\frac{3}{5}$ tornadoes were strong.

452 × $\frac{3}{10}$ = $\frac{1356}{10}$, or $135\frac{3}{5}$

$9\frac{2}{5}$ tornadoes were violent.

452 × $\frac{1}{5}$ = $\frac{452}{5}$, or $9\frac{2}{5}$

GLOSSARY

armada (ar-MAH-duh) a large force or group of moving things, usually boats

cells (SELZ) a group of clouds that can produce storms

condenses (kuhn-DENS-ez) turns from a gas into a liquid

cumulus (KUE-myoo-luss) a dense, puffy cloud with a flat base and rounded outlines

debris (duh-BREE) the scattered pieces of things that have been broken or destroyed

funnel cloud (FUHN-uhl KLOUD) a column of fast-moving air that often precedes the formation of a tornado

jet stream (JET STREEM) a band of strong, fast wind located high above Earth

ominous (AH-muh-nuhss) threatening or menacing

storm chaser (STORM CHAYSS-uhr) a person who follows the path of a tornado, hurricane, or thunderstorm in a vehicle, plane, or helicopter

supercell (SOO-puhr-sell) a powerful thunderstorm that can spin into the strongest tornadoes

twister (TWISS-tur) a tornado

underground excavation (UHN-dur-ground EK-skuh-vay-shun) a shelter or dwelling that is built in the ground

waterspout (WAH-tur-spout) a funnel-shaped column of air and water droplets that rotates over a body of water

FOR MORE INFORMATION

BOOKS

Armour, Cy. *Tornadoes and Hurricanes!* Huntington Beach, CA: Teacher Created Materials, 2011.

Fradin, Judith Bloom, and Dennis Fradin. *Tornado! The Story Behind These Twisting, Turning, Spinning, and Spiraling Storms.* Washington, DC: National Geographic, 2011.

Levete, Sarah. *Catastrophic Weather.* New York: Crabtree Publishing, 2010.

Raum, Elizabeth. *Surviving Tornadoes.* Chicago: Heinemann-Raintree, 2011.

WEB SITES

FEMA for Kids—Tornadoes
www.fema.gov/kids/tornado.htm
Check out this site from the Federal Emergency Management Agency. You'll find a guide to tornadoes and preventing disaster damage, student tornado drawings, and firsthand accounts of tornadoes written by kids.

Kids Know It Network—Tornadoes
www.kidsknowit.com/interactive-educational-movies/free-online-movies.php?movie=Tornadoes
Visit this site to view an interactive video about how tornadoes form, the Enhanced Fujita Scale, different types of tornadoes, and a fun quiz about twisters.

Weather Wiz Kids—Tornadoes
www.weatherwizkids.com/weather-tornado.htm
Watch an exciting video of tornadoes in action, conduct tornado experiments, and check out possible tornado warnings in your area.

INDEX

ABOUT THE AUTHOR

Tamra Orr is a full-time writer living in the Pacific Northwest. She has written more than 300 books for readers of all ages. Although she and her husband, four children, dog, and cat moved to Oregon in 2001, she grew up in Indiana, where tornado watches and warnings were common during the summer. She has fond memories of hiding in the basement, listening to the radio, and wondering if a tornado was sweeping through. To this day, she gets goose bumps when she hears a rumble of thunder.